CHAMPIONSHIP HABITS

#Winning in School, Work, and Life!

Adolph Brown, III

Championship Habits

#WINNING IN SCHOOL, WORK, AND LIFE

Copyright © 2018
Adolph Brown, III

The views expressed in this work are solely those of the author and do not necessarily reflect the views of the publisher, and the publisher hereby disclaims any responsibility for them. CreateSpace books may be ordered through booksellers or by contacting:
CreateSpace
4900 LaCross Road
North Charleston, SC 29406
USA

ISBN: 1547220635
ISBN: 9781547220632

DEDICATION

This book is dedicated to Don Perlyn, a devoted husband, an extraordinary father, and the esteemed results-oriented executive vice-president of Nathan's Famous, Inc. Don saw the big picture and was immensely reassuring in guiding a consultant and trainer through a steep learning curve in corporate circles long before I knew there was a book to be written.

Without Don's support and encouragement, this book would still be a twinkling in my eye and a yearning in my heart. Also by recruiting me to provide "championship habits training" for the corporate offices of Miami Subs Grille and Nathan's Famous, Inc., Don's confidence in my skills was inspiring. I would also like to thank all the organizations and corporations who have since partnered with me to learn together, to grow together, and of course WIN TOGETHER!

ACKNOWLEDGMENTS

"Successful people form the habit of doing what failures don't like to do. They like the results they get by doing what they don't necessarily enjoy."

—*Earl Nightengale*

If I presume to write about the things I believe I have seen and experienced from my vantage point, it is because I stand on the shoulders of giants. These giants have allowed me to observe the world from atop their shoulders. I thank every supervisor I have had, every corporation that employed me, and every staff person, colleague, peer, and employee who ever believed in me. I would also like to thank the giants among giants:

Dr. William R. Harvey, President, Hampton University, who role modeled Excellence in Leadership and taught me to talk and walk like a winner. He was a great persona boss who demonstrated he cared about me.

Dr. JoAnn W. Haysbert, former Provost of Hampton University and President of Langston University, who showed me that if a supervisor can stand up to you, a supervisor will also stand up for you.

Don "Cowboy for Christ" Rouse, my accountability partner who teaches me daily to make personal choices to rise above one's circumstances and exhibit the ownership necessary for achieving desired results: see it, own it, solve it, do it, and be it!

Dr. William Greer, who provided me the strongest psychoanalytic foundation possible.

Dr. Ellen Rosen, College of William and Mary, who saw something in me over two decades ago worth saving. I thank her for adding purpose to my potential.

Susan Tolley, my third grade teacher, now friend and mentor, for helping me with the "stick-to-it-iveness" needed for writing.

Beverly Outlaw, Senior Vice President Strategic Management, Sentara Norfolk General Hospital, who hired me as the Project

Manager, allowing me to make our common vision a reality for needy children and families.

Edith Jones, CEO of the STOP (Southeastern Tidewater Opportunity Project) Organization, who inspiringly refers to me as her Mandinka Warrior: never abandoning his faith, symbolizing both the tragedy of American slavery and the heroism of those who endured it.

Lee Poe (Fairfield Photography), a gentle giant in the photography industry, who captured our smiles on our wedding day, took the action photos for the cover of this book, and continues to avail himself to capture the most important moments in both our professional and private lives.

God, the creator of giants, who gifted me with phenomenal potential; I am doing my best to gift Him by putting it to great use.

These giants showed me that they cared for me and as I grow older I see that leadership styles change with times, but caring for people remains constant and can't be faked. I have evolved from being an educator who leads to being a leading educator in America.

I would like to thank my editor and friend, Terry 'TMo' Morawski, for adding my professional speaker's voice to the written word. And lastly, I thank my family for knowing me much better than others, and loving me in spite of that.

Looking forward to a relationship of LEARNING together, GROWING together, and of course...WINNING together! The life that is changed may be your own.

Adolph
June, 2018

TABLE OF CONTENTS

FOREWORD

T he story of Dr. Adolph Brown and the department of psychol-
ogy/education have become legendary inside and outside of
higher education. How did Dr. Brown offer his ideas and techniques to win his colleagues' and students' trust and eventually,
their enthusiastic commitment, to the joint goal of making his program the best in the nation?

I am delighted to write this foreword as Dr. Brown's former, and
best, supervisor ever. As Doc's (fame will cause people to shorten
your name) supervisor, I personally witnessed his secrets to creating a "winning environment;" however, not without worry. I viv-
idly recall conducting classroom observations and while peering
through the small window of the door, observing Dr. Brown walking atop the desks while lecturing. Out of respect, I chose not to
reprimand him in front of his students. I did summon him to my
office. (It was not the first time. He was almost cited by the fire
marshal the previous semester for having too many students in his
class - registered and non-registered). After I ranted on about the
safety issues pertaining to his 'balancing act,' he calmly stated that
"I can teach anyone anything, once I get their attention," he said.
"I even got yours." This is the general nature of my interactions
with Doc. **A few months later I referred to him as a modern day
"Patch Adams," he said "No, just plain ole Adolph Brown."** He
was always willing to put his program performance ahead of his
ego. I recall when he became the chair of the program; we all knew
that he would do some necessary shake-ups and shakeouts, as well
as rocking the boat. Ironically, he did, but he solicited the help of
his colleagues and students. Dr. Brown was able to have such a successful approach in the notoriously rigid hierarchy of a Historically
Black College or University (HBCU) because he employed soft
skills. He had the self-confidence to try new things and much to my
dismay, he would often create change without asking permission.
Interestingly, he always credited his students and colleagues for the
successes of the program. He knew the power of praise!

I would often tell Dr. Brown that he was a big hit among the students and faculty alike, and he would respond saying "Being liked is not as important as being respected, trusted, and effective." **Now, Dr. Brown's leadership skills were not without mistakes. For example, there was the time he arranged for a field trip he chose to call "an educational outing." By having *his entire* program involved in such an activity, it created a huge void in the lecture schedules of other programs. He did learn a lesson here. He did it again, only this time he invited the other programs.**

Some of the best program practices unique to the once largest producer of psychology/education majors in the country under Dr. Brown's leadership and tutelage included Monday night dinners at his residence for five to seven "inquisitive" students each week; personally hand-written letters of praise to the parents of meritious students; constant "budget-draining" celebrations for student and faculty accomplishments; and the introduction of catchphrases that exist today in his absence. When Dr. Brown assumed the helm, coming from the ranks as one of the youngest fully tenured university professors in the nation, the program was fledging with approximately 242 majors. He would often say at program meetings that "It is not the size of the dog in the fight, it is the size of the fight in the dog." I was always unsure if he was referring to himself as a small-statured individual, his program, or both. Needless to say, there are posters of this saying still hanging in Martin Luther King Hall on campus. During Dr. Brown's tenure, the program received two exemplary accreditation reviews; became more rigorous in design; increased to 98% graduation rate and a 91% graduate school admission rate; focused the faculty; and nearly tripled the enrollment to over 700 majors. Dr. Brown says his "4R Approach" is partly responsible for the good results...Rigor, Relevance, Relationships, and "Real Talk," also known as honest conversation amongst students and faculty. I guess Dr. Brown may know of which he writes. I am sure that I contributed to his soft skill insight via frequent approved travel to

NYC business conferences, not to forget a conference in France. (I think Mrs. Brown also had an interest in soft skills that month.)

Recently Dr. Brown confided in me (now that he has retired) that he always anticipated what I wanted before I knew it. He wanted me to not be able to get along without his program, his colleagues, and his students. He has created just that, an indispensable program with indispensable individuals. I hope his story and writings will help inspire you to rethink your soft skills philosophy.

Respectfully,

William Young, Ph.D. Dean, Graduate College
Hampton University Hampton, Virginia

INTRODUCTION

"Man's mind, once stretched by a new idea, never regains its original dimension."

—Oliver Wendell Holmes

*W*hy *all the buzz surrounding soft skills? Can anything described as soft be relevant in a corporate environment?* Soft skills are increasingly being seen as an important part of the success of an organization. Although most employees are often educated and concomitantly trained with the technical or hard skills for their professions, the soft skills complement is often absent. The term "soft skills" refers to the behaviors your mother likely reinforced when you were a child. These skills represent a cluster of personal qualities, habits, attitude and social graces that make a person a good employee or a compatible coworker. By "compatible," I mean the type of coworker who is welcome at the water cooler and a good work lunch companion. Some of us may have missed the lessons that often mark us on social graces, ability with language, personal habits, friendliness, and optimism. Parents, church leaders, and other adult role models stressed these skills during most of our childhoods. These adults have generally taught us that we could be more prosperous if we learned to use these skills. What happened? To explore this question, I spent the last ten years test-driving the wisdom of the ages, current scientific studies, and tips from popular culture.

Core Soft Skill Cluster #1

- *Possessing a strong work ethic. Are you motivated and dedicated to obtaining good results? Do you always do your best work?*

For this reason, I chose to write this short book on the issue of soft skills specifically geared toward organizations frequently dealing with customers face-to-face. Researchers have consistently found that organizations, particularly those dealing with customers face-to-face, are generally more prosperous if they train their team to use these skills. I have researched and developed 20 core soft skill clusters (personal qualities and interpersonal skills) collectively coined "championship habits" that are increasingly sought out by employers in addition to hard standard qualifications. The good news is that our parents were right!

Core Soft Skill Cluster #2

- *Possessing sociability. Are you a consensus and bridge-builder? Are you capable of navigating issues on any level – with colleagues, family, customers, and vendors? Are you likable?*

Core Soft Skill Cluster #3

- *Being responsible. Are you an accountable and a responsible individual? Are you capable of self-examination as opposed to finger pointing?*

.

CHAPTER 1

BE ALL THAT YOU WERE MEANT TO BE!

"Your vision will become clear only when you look into your heart.
Who looks outside, dreams.
Who looks inside, awakens."

—*Carl Jung*

In today's complex workplace, the 'ant colony' mentality whereby each ant performs one (and only one) task for the majority of its life is antiquated. The "bottom-line" is often the bottom-line in business. Businesses have learned that one of the easiest

Core Soft Skill Cluster #4

- *Possessing self-esteem. Will you have the courage to embrace change, ask the 'unpopular' questions, and freely contribute your ideas?*

methods to save money is to hire employees who are able to simultaneously perform a variety of separate tasks at the same time. This highly desirable behavior is commonly known as *multitasking*; however, in today's rapid changing world I will introduce the ultimate trait: *hypertasking*.

Core Soft Skill Cluster #5

- *Possessing a self-confidence. Do you believe in yourself? Do you project the confidence to inspire and the calm to settle?*

The hypertasker is the individual who is able to balance several crucial and complex tasks at once. Hypertaskers show a willingness to handle all kinds of workplace responsibilities, not just a select one or two. More importantly, these individuals display the enthusiasm for and a genuine interest in taking an active role in the success of the team and organization.

Core Soft Skill Cluster #6

- *Demonstrating time management abilities. Do you know how to effectively hypertask? Are you capable of prioritizing tasks? Will you use your time in this position wisely?*

The best aspect of being a hypertasker is the known fact that workers who branch out of their singular, well-defined roles are workers who get promoted. However, the simultaneous execution of an exceedingly large number of tasks is not without its challenges. Skillful time-management coupled with an extreme level of concentration is required to hypertask..multi-tasking to the Nth degree.

I am a huge fan of hypertasking in the appropriate contexts. I have to use this disclaimer not only as a conscientious supervisor, but also a safety-conscious parent. I am not a fan of driving while talking on the telephone, although some consider this the ultimate example of hypertasking. Like most activities we chose to participate in, there are pros and cons for each circumstance. I have listed a few pros and cons for you to apply in cases of ambiguity:

PROS: These activities are ones in which your ability to be productive does not affect the safety of you or others. An example of a pro is organizing your desk when you are placed on hold before a caller comes to the telephone. Another example is folding clothes while listening to your child's school day.

CONS: These activities are ones which serve as both unproductive as well as distracting. I have made numerous typographical errors in seemingly simple writings due to attempting to write while engaged in a telephone conversation. This con not only affects you, but you are seen as a person who is easily distracted, distant, disengaged, and disinterested. I would not recommend hypertasking during any verbal communication. When you do communicate verbally while engaged in other activities, you stand the chance of missing crucial cues, hesitations in the voice on the other end, and meaningful pauses for you to add to the conversation, for example.

It did not take my background in clinical psychology to make me keenly aware that some tasks require higher order thinking skills, and thus provide ample opportunity for error. I see numerous examples in my home whereby I will attempt to make home repairs while having a 'life talk' with one of my children. Although this example may not require much cognitive activity, I have cut boards too short, hammered my fingers more so than the nails, and stripped countless screws. My wife on the other hand, is capable of balancing our checkbook while helping our children with math. I can't imagine talking about numbers while you are writing other numbers. The distraction, for me, would be unbelievable.

We have an adage in our home that "Anything worth doing is worth doing well." After twelve years of balancing our checkbooks while ironing clothes and talking on the telephone to friends and relatives, my wife still does it better than I do, sequestered in our office away from everything and everyone.

As you sharpen your time management soft skill, be vigilant about what will suffer, if anything, as the result of your rushed pace and scattered attention. I must enter a disclaimer on behalf of my wife's phenomenal gifts in hypertasking; her gifts have been refined due to numerous years of being able to filter out distractions and use selective hearing in a home with eight children and often many of their friends.

CHAPTER 2
WHAT I DIDN'T LEARN IN GRADUATE SCHOOL

"Not in time, place, or circumstance, but in the person lies success."

—*Charles Rouce*

Unfortunately, many of us did not learn how to refine our soft skills in graduate school. Graduate schools generally do not recognize that people are good at different things and that many human traits matter in addition to academic knowledge. I believe one of the greatest lessons that many of my grad school peers and workplace colleagues have shared with me is the fact that teaching is truly hard, and being smart and well educated does not make one good at it.

I also wish I had learned that persistence and character count as much as leadership and courage. With business being conducted at an increasingly fast pace, employers are demanding individuals who are agile, adaptable, and creative at problem-solving. After perusing numerous graduate school curricula, I consistently noticed course offerings in public speaking and business writing, yet I did not observe course offerings in my 20 soft skills domains. These domains are a must for success in today's workplace. There are still lessons yet to be learned in graduate school. Explore the following while asking the subsequent questions of yourself and of your organization:

Core Soft Skill Cluster #7

- *Identifying the truth. Are you capable of sifting through the fluff and discovering what really matters? Do you have good investigatory, fact-finding, and analytic skills?*

A competitive advantage in the workplace is gained when people know how to handle themselves at work and how to relate with their customers as well as peers. Soft skills are sometimes seen as contradictory to the "strong" corporate leadership mentality and displays of "strength." The importance of showing our humanity in today's workplace far outweighs the importance of displaying toughness. Think of leaders you have worked with who showed empathy and optimism. Recall the leaders who were self-aware and vigilant about knowing what's going on outside of their corner offices.

Core Soft Skill Cluster #8

- *Demonstrating problem-solving skills. How resourceful are you? How creative are you in finding solutions?*

You probably recall a pleasant work environment that was results-oriented, although people-focused. Soft skills are a vital component to any progressive organization. Progressive individuals within organizations should remember the following simple lessons:

- Train and lead by example. Work alongside your team members from time to time.
- Inspect what you expect. Use your MBWA degree... Management By Walking Around degree.
- Catch people doing things correctly!
  Everyone likes to be complimented more than criticized.
- Only ask your team to perform activities that you would do yourself if you had to.
- Display a positive attitude during every waking hour, then dream about uplifting events while sleeping.
- Learn to fire people up and encourage them to fire themselves up.
- Quit worrying about titles. When you get good outcomes, the income and the title will follow.
- Focus on the results. Don't worry about who gets the credit for a job well done.
- Remember that winning is not everything, and losing is not terminal.
- Earn respect from your colleagues and subordinates because you can not demand it.

- Be prepared to change the play in the middle of the game.
- Celebrate success! Let people know how good you feel about them.
- Offer learning opportunities for everyone.
- Laugh out loud often...at yourself as well.

CHAPTER 3

THE CASE FOR EMOTIONAL INTELLIGENCE

"Nothing in the world can take the place of persistence. Talent will not; nothing is more common than unsuccessful men with talent. Genius will not; unrewarded genius is almost a proverb. Education will not; the world is full of educated failures. Persistence and determination alone are omnipotent."

—Calvin Coolidge

Numerous researchers posit that it is not one's intellect, skills, nor experience that makes you successful, but how well you can "read" other people's emotions and feelings in the workplace. As a former psychology professor and university dean of the graduate college, I would often explain soft skills to my students in terms of emotional intelligence (EQ) skills. Traditional management theories have missed the mark on this concept. Although we live and learn in a society that measures intelligence through quantifiable metrics both in the corporate world and public education arena, the application of EQ would prove beneficial time and time again. Just recall the *'No Child With A Behind Left Because We Are Testing It Off '* legislation. I am being facetious here. Although this legislation was designed to ensure accountability and responsibility in public education, three important questions were not asked:

- "Does every child learn the same things?"
- "Does every child learn in the same manner?"
- "Does every child learn within the same time frame?"

The answer is an emphatic "No!" A committee person with inherent soft skills could have brought this to the legislative designers' attention.

As a university chairman and dean, I was the EQ professor and EQ administrator who rewarded crisis resolution in unforeseen circumstances, demonstrated compassion to one's peers in distress, or solved an unexpected problem. I learned early on that if my students were going to be able to compete in a global society and economy, that good grades could not only be a reflection of memorizing facts and figures.

Core Soft Skill Cluster #9

- *Possessing interpersonal skills. Are you capable of teaching and mentoring others? Do you possess skills in negotiation and working with cultural diversity?*

One of the best indicators of strong emotional intelligence is the ability to work well with others on a team. Problem-solving and teamwork skills have been described as some of the most valued competencies in new hires. Every organization looks for individuals who can solve problems quickly, creatively, and of course inexpensively. The transference of the soft skills classroom training to the 'real-world' includes that of cutting budgets, to effectively handling crises, and meeting seemingly impossible deadlines, to name a few. In fact, I would train all of my students to answer the following open-ended question during a senior seminar course:

"Tell me about a time when you faced a tough problem. How did you solve it?"

Core Soft Skill Cluster #10

- *Possessing social skills. Are you able to deal with the emotions of others? Do you have the abilities to harmonize, persuade, and lead?*

I would share with my students that an interview is a perfect place to display your numerous soft skills. There is hard evidence that soft skills are the major factor in developing a high-performing team or organization. An analysis of more than 300 top-level executives from 15 global companies showed that six emotional competencies distinguish the best and brightest from the average: Influence, Team Leadership, Organizational Awareness, Self-Confidence, Achievement Drive, and Leadership. Researchers have also demonstrated an exciting correlation between a leader's personal characteristics and leadership competencies with her personal, team, and organization performance.

Improving one's emotional intelligence should start with a psycho-behavioral concept I developed while I was in graduate school. One must focus in three areas:

- Internal self-language, also called "self-talk"
- One's attitude or belief system that predisposes them to act in certain ways
- Consequential resulting behaviors or actions.

My theory is commonly known as L-A-B, whereby **L**anguage drives **A**ttitude, and attitude contributes to an overt manifestation of **B**ehavior. Simply put, in order to master emotional intelligence, one must reframe his internal voice or thoughts, develop skill sets, and experiment with new behaviors and master feelings. I have seen countless examples where the use of my cognitive behavioral therapy L-A-B techniques based in sound psychodynamic principles have enhanced emotional intelligence for corporate CEOs and other executives, educators, military personnel, counselors, consultants, mental health professionals and husbands/wives. One major reason life coaches and consultants are so popular within the business world is that we help individuals to step back from the movie of their life in order to review and reset their thinking and actions.

CHAPTER 4
ATTITUDE IS STILL EVERYTHING

"By becoming more aware, perhaps…perhaps we can also, in that way, refrain from adding our personal darkness to the shadow."

—*Zweig and Abrams*

Core Soft Skill Cluster #11

- *Demonstrating a positive attitude. Are you optimistic, enthusiastic, and upbeat? Are you capable of generating positive energy and good will?*

In today's service oriented global economy which focuses on the ascendance of work teams in organizations, a new premium is placed on soft skills, people skills, relationship-building, and the essence of a positive attitude. Your attitude or the way you think, day in and day out, is the most pervasive soft skill, affecting every aspect of your life.

Core Soft Skill Cluster #12

- *Having the ability to accept and learn from criticism.*
  Are you coachable? Are you capable of continuous learning and improvement?

One common characteristic of successful individuals is that they have learned to precede their actions with positive self-talk. Language is the software of the mind. William Shakespeare is quoted (*Hamlet II, ii, 259*): "There is nothing either good or bad, but thinking it makes it so." I often say "There is no good or bad, what matters is how hard you try." For some, trying to have a positive attitude is quite challenging. Their internal dialogue is negative and adversely affects the way they behave (**L-A-B**). The great news about internal dialogue is that we can learn to listen to the voice and recognize faulty thought patterns. You are in control of your own thoughts, unless you believe that aliens possess power and control over you. This belief would definitely require a different book. As the old adage goes, "It isn't necessarily bad to talk to yourself; it just depends on what you are saying." Thoughts like, "I could never do that," "I am not good enough," and "What if I fail?' serve as cues to change scripts immediately. We have to silence the inner critic in us and cease the internal voice of negative judgmental self talk. The inner critic separates us from our best self as well as from others. Self- imposed negativity and judgment spills over to our interactions with others and often negatively contaminates all that we do, touch, and experience. It is critically important to choose your words carefully when you 'talk to yourself.'

In organizations, negative attitudes serve to distance others and erode relationships. Individuals who are incapable of escaping negative thoughts become *basement people* as described by famous psychoanalyst Sigmund Freud. Freud describes *basement people* as those who have such a negative outlook that everything in their life appears dismal and unsatisfying. An example of a basement person in your organization would be one on the dysfunctional "R.O.A.D. program" also known as Retirement On Active Duty. *Basement people* spend the majority of their time looking for opportunities to be offended. *Basement people* do not like to see others pursue their dreams and aspirations because it serves as a reminder of how far they are from their own.

On the opposite end of the spectrum, Freud describes *balcony people* as those who appreciate the positive elements of their own personalities and the best qualities in others. *Balcony people* are the personal success coaches who empathically and tirelessly encourage others. *Balcony people* are "dream boosters," not "dream busters." We all have the capacity to be balcony people as well as to employ inner voices of affirmation.

Discover your primary and favorite mode of conversation in the workplace. Are you gossiping and complaining about people and situations? Do you always look for the bad and worse in others? Also be aware of how you are being reinforced...most people will only give you a couple of minutes of their time when you are really excited and happy, but if you are wallowing in sorrow, you can always find someone to chat with for hours.

Even from a health and wellness perspective, you function better when you feel good. A positive attitude leads to improved energy levels, immune system effectiveness, mental and emotional clarity, and enjoyment of a better overall quality of life. Start catch-ing your negative thoughts and reframing them towards positive affirmations. Remember that 'we become what we think about.' It has also been said that the quality of one's life is directly correlated to the quality of one's thoughts.

CHAPTER 5

TAKE CARE OF YOUR CUSTOMERS OR SOMEONE ELSE WILL

"You can't build a reputation on what you are going to do."

—*Henry Ford*

Core Soft Skill Cluster #13

- *Listening effectively to your customers and colleagues. Are you an active listener with pause and silences, mirroring, disclosing, and appropriate questioning? Are you able to observe verbal and nonverbal cues?*

Most, if not all customers, appreciate a "willingness to help" and the fact that "she listened to my complaint." The use of this soft skill is a key factor in today's business dealings. It separates and often elevates your organization above the competition. There is a common misperception in the business world that we compete only with products. Successful and progressive organizations know that their people are the source of their power. By focusing on the people within your organization, you must also be careful not to overemphasize expertise and credentials. The values and basics of good internal and external customer service are still paramount. Treat all customers, both potential and loyal, as if they have a sign hanging around their neck that reads "Make me feel important!" It appears that we have been conducting business by a perversion of The Golden Rule, "Do unto others before they do unto you." Even in advertising, some corporations have adopted the behavior "Do the consumers before the competitors do them." Regardless of the nature of the medium, quality customer service depends on the self-concept of both partners in the exchange. With this understanding, employers would experience tremendous gains after learning to fire employees up as opposed to just firing employees. Think of the customer service soft skills set as the Triple A approach (Attention, Affirmation, and Appreciation). By Triple A, I mean three words that start with "A," and not any reference to the largest motor club association in the United States. The Golden Psychological Rule applies to the Triple A Approach, "We do to others what we do to ourselves," or simply put, "We treat others the way we treat ourselves."

Soft skills can and do trademark companies for professionalism and customer service. I have yet to enter a well-known establishment, public schools included, that does not have a strategically placed written statement referencing who they are, what they stand for, and what they will do for you. This is a basic difference in cookie-cutter organizations and those that strive for customer loyalty. Customer satisfaction is the key as noted in the national findings across numerous industries, including findings by the National Federation of Independent Business (NFIB):

- Sixty-five percent of a company's business comes from existing customers.
- It costs five times as much to attract a new customer than to keep an existing one.
- It takes twelve good service experiences to overcome one bad service experience.
- Twenty-five percent of customers cite poor service (not price or quality) as the reason for not returning.
- Ninety-one percent of unhappy customers will never buy AGAIN from a company that displeased them.
- Unhappy customers will complain to nine outside people.
- Satisfied customers will tell five people about their positive experience.
- Customers who complain and have their complaints satisfied are likely to be loyal customers to your business.
- Every customer has a lifetime value and should receive that type and level of treatment.
- Quality and delivery of service are a few variables that can distinguish a business from its competition.
- GOOD SERVICE LEADS TO INCREASED SALES!

There is no shortage of demanding employees and insatiable customers in today's working environment. Organizations simply cannot survive without a loyal customer base. Researchers commonly state that it can take a lifetime to secure a loyal customer and only a few seconds to lose one. Organizations can not operate without committed employees and loyal customers. With the acquisition of soft skills, organizations can effectively recruit and retain customers by utilizing the charm of their employees' appeal over the concrete technical skills.

CHAPTER 6
TALK AND WALK LIKE A WINNER

"It's a funny thing about life; if you refuse to accept anything but the best, you very often get it."

—*Somerset Maugham*

It is an important realization that no matter how big your brain is or how much you know, your wealth of knowledge will be a secret until you are able to effectively communicate with others. It should be common knowledge that we are often judged by how we present ourselves and how we speak. Some cultures have grasped this quicker than others. Although some researchers have begun to demonstrate that black men are lacking in the soft skills related to their motivation and ability to interact well with customers and coworkers, *all* groups can stand to benefit from the lessons put forth in this chapter. The ability to succeed or fail based on soft skills is the same, no matter your gender, ethnicity, or background.

Core Soft Skill Cluster #14

- *Possessing the ability to self-manage. Are you capable of self-reflection and introspection? Are you capable of mood management?*

Due to heightened competitive pressure in the workplace, soft skills are becoming increasingly more important. This helps explain some of the growing disadvantages experienced by some groups in today's labor market. Talking and walking like a winner entails practicing how to communicate correctly both verbally and nonverbally. It involves being keenly aware of what your body language, choice of clothing, and outward/physical appearance says about you. How are you being interpreted by others? By successfully learning the art of presenting yourself well, you will always be able to sell yourself for what you are really worth. On the flip side, people begin making judgments about you be- fore you ever open your mouth. So, be sure everything about how you present yourself matches the amazing person inside.

As I often referred to in my book, *This is Real Talk,* students and professionals must be reminded that there is a time and a place for everything. For a man to show up to a job interview with pants that 'sag' or a woman to show up wearing pants that fit too tightly basically says that you do not understand the above-mentioned cliché nor workplace expectations. Understanding "code-switching" is essential for success, especially for minorities. Code-switching is not just a linguistic term referring to using more than one language or variety in a conversation, it also refers to matching the appropriate behavior with the appropriate setting – i.e. "When in Rome, we act as the Romans do..." Also, from my *Real Talk* book, I remind minority students either entering the business world or adjusting to it, not to worry about being seen as a *"sellout."* More importantly, they should concern themselves with *'outselling'* everyone in the business. I have long since vowed to think of myself as a winner, and as a result, I surround myself with winners. I simply can not overstate how much this influenced my life, encouraged my forward thinking, and shaped my attitudes about business. To emphasize talking and walking like a winner, I have a few basic, but proven suggestions for the acquisition of these soft skills.

- Always look people in their eyes when speaking to them.
- If you do not understand something, ask for clarification.
- Stay away from 'lazy language' (e.g., "gonna," "wanna").
- Project and practice confidence by using good posture.
- Speak slowly and clearly.
- Learn how to effectively speak in public. (Glossophobia, or the fear of public speaking, is the most common phobia in the U.S.)
- Surround yourself with people smarter than you.
- Know your limitations.
- Shake hands firmly.

- Wear clothes that fit you.
- Be sure to smile. A smile is a small curve that often straightens things out.

As you begin to talk and walk like a winner, you will be seen as displaying championship habits!

CHAPTER 7

DIFFERENTIATION OF LEADERS AND MANAGERS

"Rather than being the illness, the symptoms are the beginning of its cure. The fact that they are unwanted makes them all the more a phenomenon of grace, a message to initiate self-examination and repair."

—M. Scott Peck

The terms 'manager' and 'leader' are not synonomous. Peter Drucker and Warren Bennis, two notable names in the business field, say "Leadership is doing the right things; management is doing things right." Soft skills are obviously significant as the leader's primary role is to form a new focus for an organization, whereas a manager's role is to help fulfill that vision. It is important to understand that technical competence is necessary, but having the people skills to communicate vision is vital.

Core Soft Skill Cluster #15

- *Demonstrating good communication skills. Are you able to express ideas with clarity?*

The best examples of this differentiation can be best explained in public education. The principal of a school is a "manager" by professional description, and not necessarily a leader. As a manager, the school administrator oversees the day-to-day operations and activities. However, if the principal desires for her staff, students, and parents to willingly follow her and put their trust in her, then she must also be a leader.

As a leader, the school administrator attempts to see how she can shape the future of the school and what new initiatives they can employ to do so.

Researchers have demonstrated that although people are more loyal to leaders than to managers, in order to effectively deal with one's subordinates, school administrators must be in touch with their 'softer side' or soft skills. Principals must be intuitively aware of the strengths and weaknesses of all team players. For example, if a teacher is found to be soft and kind, it would be obvious that this teacher would work better with younger children rather than with teenagers. Some of the worst examples of management without leadership can be seen when a native English-speaking history teacher is requested to teach English simply because she is available and can speak the language. The school administrator who employs her soft skills will only ask teachers to teach classes which relate to their specialty or content area understanding that knowing a subject does not necessarily translate into being able to teach it. Often it is overlooked that businesses that do a good job of selecting, training, and developing their staff will enjoy higher productivity and lower turnover. While some researchers (not this one) believe that it is difficult to measure the impact soft skills have on productivity, it is certainly obvious that staff who feel good about working for an organization or supervisor will want to contribute much more than the minimum acceptable level.

Core Soft Skill Cluster #16
- *Possessing integrity and honesty. Do you have good character or behave in ways consistent with a strong value system? Do you practice and apply sound ethical principles?*

In my consultative activities throughout the years, I have seen some of the best school administrators exemplify the highest standards of both managerial and leadership qualities. These principals take the blame when things go wrong and understand that "when things go wrong, not to go with them." These principals field complaints from their "customers," the parents, by acknowledging any mistakes that they might have made, and DO NOT blame the teachers. The best 'managing leader' principals also give credit where it is due. They know how to motivate the staff to be more involved in the school's future. Ultimately, in my mind, the public schools' model is quite similar to that of business industry. Just as in business, celebrating major achievements creates a tone of positivity and creates a climate of teamwork. And synonomous to every successful business, the best school administrators are "empowerers" who delegate the day-to-day activities in order to focus on planning for the school's future.

Although the roles of manager and leader require soft skills, it is the role of the leader, 'the chief climate-shaper,' to establish the structures, conditions, and attitudes through which a manager oversees getting things done. The best method to determine if you are a manager, a leader, or both, is to ask yourself if you can create positive change. A manager can maintain a direction, but is often unable to change it. Both managers and leaders must be keenly aware of the players who comprise their teams. They must remember to acknowledge and recognize team members for the unique talents and gifts they bring to bear.

As an example of championship habits, would Phil Jackson, as the once-leader of the Chicago Bulls have given the same job description and expect the same results from former teammates Scottie Pippin and Michael Jordan? The answer is easy because we can understand the concept that each professional athlete lends a different contribution to the overall success of the team.

When managers and leaders are able to interchange roles in today's rapidly changing work environment, team success is often just over the horizon. However, it is critical that one understand when to switch gears. To put it simply: when managing, begin with people (looking inward at the organization); when leading, begin with the picture of where you are headed (looking out- ward).

CHAPTER 8

HOW TO PUT SOFT SKILLS INTO HARDWIRED ENVIRONMENTS

"Come to the edge," he said. They said, "We are afraid."
"Come to the edge," he said. They came. He pushed
them…and they flew."

—*Guilliaume Appollinaire*

As your organization strives to reach its full potential, remember to maintain absolute integrity. Role model confidence while promoting and supporting content, show uncommon commitment, expect the best from all, and most importantly, ask the right questions.

Core Soft Skill Cluster #17

- *Possessing the ability to be a team player. Are you cooperative when working in groups? Are you both comfortable being a leader and allowing another to take the lead?*

Asking the right questions should evolve from the basic tenets of the following questions:

1. What motivates you and your employees? **Beware of the assumption that all people are motivated by the same things. People are motivated by a whole range of factors including financial rewards, status, praise and acknowledgment, competition, job security, public recognition, perfectionism, results, freedom, autonomy, etc. Also be cognizant of who is most motivated and why.**
2. What prevents you and your employees from exemplary performance? **Be sure to find out about demotivating factors in the workplace as well as in the personal lives of you and your employees.**
3. Do you and your employees feel empowered? **Are you and your employees treated as robots...basically given a list of tasks to perform and simply told what to do? Make sure you and your employees have some autonomy that allows people to find their own solutions.**
4. How do you and your employees feel about the organization? Do you and your employees feel safe, valued, loyal,

and taken care of? **Be vigilant to feelings of being taken advantage of, dispensable, and invisible. Once these feelings are detected, be sure to eradicate them immediately! Ask yourself and your employees what would improve overall loyalty and commitment.**

We often forget that to make a difference, we have to sometimes be different. To be truly "outstanding," we will have to be willing to "stand out." Standing out in front of the parade has its benefits, but it also leaves you vulnerable to be kicked in the pants. As you move forward, remember to take care of your people. If you do, then your people will protect you as well.

- **Empower your employees**. Give them the authority and responsibility of satisfying, creating, and retaining loyal customers.
- **Train your employees**. Train, train, and then retrain your employees with the tools to strive for excellence in their roles.
- **Market your service**. Marketing should communicate that your employees are also your customers and you will do everything in your power to keep them satisfied.
- **Hire good people**. OQP...Only Quality People!
- **Measure job performance**. What gets measured gets done!
- **Get feedback from your employees and other customers**. Listen carefully to suggestions and implement as many as possible. Always welcome criticism.
- **Strive to be fair and consistent**. Consistency enhances credibility and reliability.
- **Know your competition**. Once you know, then do it better!
- **Accept only excellence**. High expectations drive high achievement.
- **Go the extra mile**. Under promise and over deliver!

CHAPTER 9
THE HARD CASE FOR SOFT SKILLS

"Accept human differences and limitations. Don't expect anyone to be perfect. Remember, the other person has a right to be different. And don't be a reformer."

—David Schwartz

The global economy requires organizations to be comfortable in embracing differences, particularly among cultures. To go a step further is to 'get out of one's comfort zone' and truly take advantage of the inherent value in relationship-building. Significant relationships will always precede significant results. I have noticed numerous underperforming organizations in the global environment, including public schools and universities. We often believe people are the same everywhere and expect everyone to behave like us. In a global environment, it is essential to work with individuals, groups, and organizations that are unlike our own.

To effectively maximize one's global efforts, the following soft skills must be utilized:

- An understanding that differences exist and matter
- An openness and receptiveness to new and different ideas and ways of doing things
- A genuine appreciation of how behaviors differentiate

There will always be some who remain unconvinced of the value of soft skills. I have found that managers with minimal leadership qualities who prefer to focus on being bottom-line driven, strategists, technical experts, and "snoopervisors" tend to think soft skills are a lot of "fluff." Case in point: as the economy grows, so must our understanding of relationships with our employees and partners here and overseas. As we continue to move forward in our corporate globalization efforts, we must educate students and professionals to employ more flexibility in their thinking and learn to appreciate incorporating different perspectives. Soft skills deal with the world of emotions and feelings that are critical to the success of any organization or team.

<u>Core Soft Skill Cluster #18</u>

- *Demonstrating flexibility and adaptability. Are you able to adapt as well as **overcome** obstacles in new situations and challenges? Are you open to new ideas and ways of thinking about things?*

Organizations should also know when to seek assistance. As a coach and organizational consultant, I have created a team of experts in framing the issues, building rapport, and establishing the right culture for initiatives to blossom. I have yet to meet an individual or organization who does not like winning. Remember, whether you are already working in the business world, applying for a position, or even employed in a technical position, it's your combination of core and soft skills that will set you apart from the crowd! Continue to use the points in this short read to create uncontested global market space for yourself whereby making your competition irrelevant!

CHAPTER 10
A SENSE OF ENTITLEMENT

*"We can only be said to be alive in those moments when
our hearts are conscious of our treasures."*

—*Thornton Wilder*

A sense of entitlement is the newest problem that I believe is ruining our homes, our culture, and especially our workplaces. Have you ever witnessed persons for whom nothing you do is ever good enough and they rarely show appreciation for the efforts demonstrated by others...on their behalf? It is not just a teenager issue anymore to expect the best of everything despite a lack of effort and parents' financial realities. This type of "stinking thinking" has infected our workplaces. In the human relations field of psychology, a sense of entitlement is an outrageous attitude of narcissistic individuals who believe the world "owes" them and they are always looking to collect. It has been almost commonplace to hear the following poisoned attitudes in organizations across the country:

"What's in it for me?" WIIFM sense of entitlement radio
"What have you done for me lately?" An R&B track
played continuously on WIIFM
"This company owes me! Performance does not matter."
"I put in my eight hours, what more do you expect me to
do?" Like small children, many adults whine at the slight-
est inconvenience, restriction, delay, challenge, or
just anything not suited to their comfort. In hard times,
the economic threats that face the United States, unfair
trade, or illegal immigration, do not adversely affect our
culture as badly as a sense of entitlement of some
Americans. There is an eagerness for some to shift the
blame when things do not go according to plan. One
must take responsibility for the personal decisions one
makes. I was recently reminded of the sense of entitlement
problem while reading an article on numerous
professional athletes who have salaries at fifty times that of
the educators who helped them get to that level as well
as having an infinite number of opportunities. Yet, many
professional athletes take these conditions for granted

They forget that they have jobs with subsequent job descriptions, responsibilities, roles, and performance evaluations. Just think for a moment if you, a regular Joe, got into a physical altercation or a fight while at work (with a co-worker or a supervisor), failed countless drug tests, showed reckless abandon for laws, or lacked the character to represent your organization in the best of lights? Needless to say, you would probably become unemployed. How is it that professional athletes believe that workplace decorum and etiquette does not apply to them? It's the result of a huge sense of entitlement. I am of the belief that these athletes do not need more money to take to the banks, but more lectures to take to heart. My grandfather once told me that life was not fair, but I should do my best anyway. I now say, "The only fair in life is a carnival."

We have to rid our homes, our culture, and especially our workplaces of the "you owe me" mentality. This premise is faulty and leads to one habitually blaming others for one's troubles. The following core soft skill requires one to be "response-able" or capable of having the ability to improve one's situation by responding differently.

Core Soft Skill Cluster #19

- *Demonstrating accountability and responsibility for your behavior, attitude, and fate. Do you possess a victim's mentality or an attitude of survivor's pride? Are you capable of an "attitude of gratitude?"*

Becoming a response-able individual involves active participation in your life. You can choose your attitude basically asserts that circumstances are beyond your control but you can choose how to react to them. More specifically regarding soft skills, the work you do may be out of your control; however, you can choose whether or not to enjoy it. It is quite interesting that many of us today decide how good of a work day we have based on the effectiveness and efficiency of the technology we use. It is likely that today's technology-dependent culture will be at a significant disadvantage if we do not add a soft skill every time we add a new technovation or electronic age convenience; i.e. cell phone, PDA, iPOD, GPS, email, etc.

C.P. Snow was quoted in the March 15, 1971 edition of the *New York Times* stating, "Technology...is a queer thing. It brings you great gifts with one hand, and it stabs you in the back with the other." Is technology changing our value system? Remember when driving alongside of an automobile with children as passengers? One could observe children counting cars, observing nature, playing 'punch buggy,' or engaged in seemingly meaningful conversation. Nowadays, children are watching television behind the headrests of the front seats as they travel. In an age where technology is attempting to surpass our humanity, we must pay close attention to focus on the people we are grateful for in life.

An attitude of gratitude can be found by simply focusing on the parts of your life that you are most thankful for. Work-wise, being thankful can give you a fresh perspective and bring you into the present during a hectic and overwhelming day. I have learned that it is difficult to be able to feel sad and thankful at the same time. It is also great to feel thankful for someone else's success or their contribution to you. Researchers show that grateful people have higher reported levels of the positive states of alertness, enthusi-asm, determination, attentiveness, and energy. Choosing your at-titude is making a conscious effort not to behave like a victim of specific technologies, clients, team members, or supervisors.

CHAPTER 11
THE BIG DANCE

"Whatever you think you can do or believe you can do, begin it. Action has magic, grace, and power in it."

—*Goethe*

D ance is one of my favorite metaphors for change, active life participation, and certainly living life to its fullest. Dancing is a participatory activity and often individuals are reluctant to "bust a move." When my friends tell me that they do not dance because of lack of rhythm, I remind them that if their heart is still beating…then they have rhythm. Dancing is just like every organization: you can't go up while sitting down. Even if you

Core Soft Skill Cluster #20

- *Working well under pressure. Can you effectively handle stress and deadlines? Are you capable of being a pinch-hitter and producing your best work?*

are uncomfortable with change, wouldn't you agree that life is far too fragile not to occasionally try something new and different? *Get out of the box* and attempt to be nonconformal and creative. Soft skills really lend themselves to my dance metaphor; as dancing does not require much (or any) technical knowledge, it only requires those skills pertinent to our workplaces known as confidence, willingness to move, and the ability to laugh at yourself from time to time.

Like in the business world, there are a few implicit assumptions you'll need to get acquainted with when dancing. It is imperative that you throw caution to the wind in this endeavor with the understanding that failure is not the most pleasant aspect of the 'success dance,' but it is definitely a necessary ingredient. The primary rules surround…sometimes you lead, other times you follow, but you always attempt to match the steps of the person with whom you are dancing. If you experience failure, mishaps, or missteps in your dance, it is just a sign to change directions, paths, or course. Often times this lesson serves to teach you new dances for new opportunities. Timing is another minute factor in dancing; however, it is becoming less important in our Internet-savvy world. It was once crucial to be 'the first on the dance floor,' or the first to pilot a study or to implement a new concept or idea. Nowadays, it is actually better to implement the second-best idea with all the kinks of the first worked out. Don't settle for only playing the hand you were dealt and accepting this as your life. Lead your life incorporating soft skills at every turn...ensuring that your work and workplace are rewarding, profitable, and a quality experience! Hear the music and keep on dancing.

In the words of Lee Ann Womack:

I hope you never lose your sense of wonder,
You get your fill to eat but always keep that hunger,
May you never take one single breath for granted,
God forbid love ever leave you empty handed,
I hope you still feel small when you stand beside the ocean,
Whenever one door closes I hope one more opens
Promise me that you' ll give faith a fighting chance,
And when you get the choice to sit it out or dance,

I hope you dance...I hope you dance.

Tough Times Never Last, But Tough People Do!

Book Doc

For Your Upcoming Event!

"Winning is not everything, but making the effort to win is."

—Vince Lombardi

Invite Dr. Adolph Brown to speak, consult, or coach for your organization at

www.docspeaks.com.

Be Sure To Have Doc as Your Organization's
Mystery Guest.

Excellence is Sure to Follow!

Your employees will definitely **HEAR THE MUSIC** *and LEARN* **TO DANCE** *with a visit from Doc. www.docspeaks.com*

"This book is a must-read to assist in developing the ability to relate the social and occupational relations that cover the vital but little understood element of customer motivation and its application to any product or service that is being sold. Adolph Brown is the true champion."

—Frank Turner Regional Manager Zale Corporation

"I really enjoyed and was very much intrigued by how many of these concepts apply to home and professional life. I will use this emotionally intelligent book as a quick personal and professional reference to continually reinforce my softer side."

—K. Yost
General Manager
Huntington Beach, CA

"This book was extremely informative, and now I am more mo- tivated and excited to be a better manager and top leader. I am ready to go back to my company and try to make it a better workplace. My eyes are now opened to improve my own skills as well."

Ben Filson
Team Leader
Flowery Branch, GA

"Absolutely invaluable to me in my new career. By taking the advice in your book, I am now on the escalator to success. This was the single best professional investment I have made in a long time. You are truly a great soul and you give much more than information, your words and deeds are so inspiring."

Dr. Sarah Jacobson
Phoenix, AZ

"Adolph Brown is a champion who makes others into champi- ons. He has excelled as a full tenured university professor, award winning administrator, corporate project manager, pole-vaulter, martial artist, training facilitator, professional speaker, and author. He has shaped the lives of students (elementary through college) and professionals from all walks of life into championship people. He daily transforms championship hearts into champion- ship habits. He is a life changing Master Teacher in every sense of the word!"

Andy Lilburn Projects Manager Elmhurst, NY

Made in the USA
Columbia, SC
24 October 2018